WINNING

THE

WAR

ON

WORRY

WINNING THE WAR ON WORRY

*CULTIVATE A PEACEFUL HEART
AND A CONFIDENT MIND*

LOUIE GIGLIO

W Publishing Group
An Imprint of Thomas Nelson

Winning the War on Worry: Cultivate a Peaceful Heart and a Confident Mind

© 2022 Louie Giglio

Published in Nashville, Tennessee, by W Publishing, an imprint of Thomas Nelson.

Thomas Nelson titles may be purchased in bulk for educational, business, fundraising, or sales promotional use. For information, please email SpecialMarkets@ThomasNelson.com.

ISBN 978-1-4003-3370-7 (SC)
ISBN 978-1-4003-3372-1 (Audio)
ISBN 978-1-4003-3371-4 (ePub)

Library of Congress Cataloging-in-Publication Data

2022940737

Printed in the United States of America

22 23 24 25 26   LSC   10 9 8 7 6 5 4 3 2 1

CONTENTS

WELCOME TO A NEW WAY OF LIFE

By the simple fact that you chose to crack open the first page of this book—*Winning the War on Worry*—I'm assuming you might be worried right now. Sure, it's possible you could just be checking out this little book "for a friend." Or maybe you're one of the few select people on earth who hasn't experienced any of the warring tensions of worry and anxiety. But I'm thinking that if you're holding these pages in your hands, it's more likely you want to worry less. Which is exactly what this resource is intended to help you do.

Worry is so prevalent in our society and throughout our daily lives that it often feels inescapable. Instead of worry being an occasional event, many of us have learned to embrace worry as a part of the fabric of our lives. Worry has become woven into our regular rhythms, and for many of us, it's become an identity. We say, "I'm a worrier. It's just the way I am." As a result, we live in a perpetual state of being worried about something. In fact, you might already be worried about the promise and prospect of this book.

Will it work for me?
Will it be a waste of my time?
Should I have chosen something different to read?
Will I be able to finish this book and get through each chapter?

Like barnacles on the bottom of a boat, worry has a way of subtly attaching itself to our thoughts. Worry often starts below the waterline, out of sight, out of the forefront of our thoughts. At first it's just a simple *what if . . .*

What if I get to the reception late and miss the moment?
What if I don't know anyone when I get there?
What if my supervisor hates my idea?
*What if it rains next week on the night I've planned the
    outdoor party?*

Before you know it worrying becomes a way of life. And just like those barnacles on the bottom of a boat add weight and resistance and therefore slow down the vessel, worry slows down your progress and corrodes your quality of life.

Over time, these little *what ifs* that we allow to creep in and stick to the hull of our hearts begin to morph into substantial and sinking fears. Even before a *what if* ever comes to fruition, the more we allow it to linger and feed it with our attention and activity, the more it begins to weigh us down. As believers, we are meant to live a life characterized by the light and easy yoke of Jesus (Matthew 11:30), and the more room we give *what ifs*, the more heavily burdened we become.

Maybe for you, the list of *what-if* questions above seemed slightly trivial. You might have read through those statements and said, "Louie, I've got bigger concerns on my radar than what the weather is going to look like next week." I hear that. My wife, Shelley, and I are also walking through some difficult circumstances with our family right now. But even in the hardest moments, that element of *what if* remains the same. Maybe your *what if* looks a little more like this:

What if there's an accident?

What if I'm one of the employees who gets let go at work?

What if I'm not up to the task and I fail?

What if I'm not really saved?

What if my child rebels?

What if my friend bails out on me?

What if my spouse leaves me?

What if I get cancer?

What if this is the end of the world?

Arthur Somers Roche said so well: "Worry is like a thin stream of fear trickling through the mind. If encouraged, it cuts a channel into which all other thoughts are drained."[1]

---

1. Thomas E. Trask and Wayde I. Goodall, *The Fruit of the Spirit* (Nashville, TN: Thomas Nelson, 2018).

Before we go too much further, let's pause to clarify something right away. You are not the only person to step onto this battlefield and look across the way toward the enemy of worry and anxiety. The Enemy loves to isolate us and make our struggles seem disproportionate to those around us. But worry isn't an uncommon tactic. In fact, it's one of the Enemy's go-to weapons. There is some level of comfort in knowing that worry strikes people from every walk of life and background.

Worry can weasel into the hearts of business leaders, professional athletes, high-school seniors, first-time moms, creatives and artists and producers and designers and software engineers. It can creep into the minds of chefs and astronauts, truck drivers and teachers. It can even get into the minds of pastors and people who are called to work for the church.

I have to admit—I've spent a lot of my life worrying. I used to blame it on the fact that I come by it naturally, given that my mom and dad were Olympic-caliber worriers.

But here's the stunning truth: worry is a choice.

When I say that, I'm not being simplistic. This isn't my

attempt to smooth over rough waters with a pithy statement or a few cheap words. It's based on my personal experience and the truth I've seen over and over throughout the Word of God.

In my previous books I've been very open about my struggles with anxiety and depression, and I know full well that there's no one-size-fits-all solution to our varied struggles. I also know that catchy slogans don't solve mental illness. Yet, God has lifted me up out of a pretty deep and dark place. He brought me back into the light to proclaim—God is greater. He and He alone can calm stormy waters. He can speak a word that makes the winds and waves subside.

God can conquer worry because He has already been victorious over the ultimate root of worry: fear. We'll dig into this in a later chapter, but 1 John 4:18 says it so well: "There is no fear in love. But perfect love drives out fear."

God is greater than fear and all its cousins—depression, anxiety, panic, and worry. And if God is greater, you and I can experience freedom from the grip of worry that robs us of sleep and peace.

I believe that as we go through these next chapters

together, the truths you encounter will have the potential to set you on a new path and give you the tools you need to replace worry with a greater sense of trust in the Almighty. It's time to take a good, hard look at the root of worry that has grown and spread throughout our hearts. It's time we examine the deep levels of our souls and begin to weed out this way of living as we reclaim a peaceful heart and a confident mind.

Throughout our journey together, we'll look at both the theological and the practical. We'll fix our eyes on the only One who has perfectly conquered worry and anxiety, while also setting our feet into motion as we go to war on worry. If you stick with this, I believe you will find help for the headache and hardship lingering in your life. However, please understand, this is no *self-help* guide.

The essence of winning the war on worry is knowing you can't do it on your own. Like most attacks of the Enemy, when we battle worry, we can't make or muster a strong enough defense by ourselves. It is only by the might of God and the love of Jesus that we can stand firm, take ground, and win this fight.

My goal is to point you to the One who is greater—to the God who encourages His people:

> Don't worry about anything; instead, pray about everything. Tell God what you need, and thank him for all he has done. Then you will experience God's peace, which exceeds anything we can understand. His peace will guard your hearts and minds as you live in Christ Jesus. (Philippians 4:6–7 NLT)

So join me as we begin this journey of repelling worry from our hearts. It's a big fight, but the great reality is that every big fight can start with a small, simple step. Picking up this book is an example of that first small step. By opening these pages, you are saying, "I need something to change," and that is a powerful place to start.

So before we get into the thick of it, before we even jump in to chapter 1, let's pause here at the very beginning and take a step together. Remember when I said that the Enemy loves to utilize the weapon of *what if*? Instead of fixating on the *what ifs*, let's commit right now to acknowledging that God has already provided us with the truth of *what is*. God doesn't deal in confusion. He doesn't leave things to chance, and He is never unsure of the final outcome. He doesn't do *if*. He *is*—and that is a truth on which we can build our foundation.

So wherever you are reading this, no matter what you are walking through, I encourage you to speak out this reality: *God, I believe You are greater. Specifically, You are greater than whatever I am worrying about right now.*

I believe this confession will immediately catalyze the process of resizing worry and replacing it with trust.

And if you're not quite able to declare those words with full conviction, then maybe this is your confession: *God, help me have greater faith in You.* This is a prayer God loves to hear and loves to come through for.

If you're ready to live free, to cultivate a peaceful heart and confident mind, He's ready to help you bury worry and live with a new reality of deep-rooted trust and hope.

ONE

WORRY IS A LIAR

We've already established that the root of worry is fear. And fear doesn't come from God. Thus, at the heart of worry is the devil. And Scripture is clear—the devil is a liar.

Jesus said about him: "When he lies, he speaks his native language, for he is a liar and the father of lies" (John 8:44).

To put it simply, worry isn't just a bad habit. Worry is an Enemy tactic—a strategy built on lies that are designed to rob you of peace and tear your mind to pieces.

That's why it's crucial that you are able to spot the lies worry tells.

Not long ago while on safari in South Africa, Shelley

and I were really wanting to see a leopard in the wild. Early and late on our game drives our eyes were set on every tree limb, bush, grassy hill, and river path in hopes of finding one of several leopards that were known to frequent this particular area. But here's the thing: leopards aren't bright orange with tall, sparkly antennae on their backs. They are designed to blend into the surroundings, like the bark of a baobab tree where they might be lounging on one of its mighty branches.

In the same way, the devil isn't going to jump up and down in front of you shouting, "Hey, I'm a liar, and everything I'm telling you right now is going to drain your life of joy!" No, he's going to arrive more acceptably—in the form of worry. Because everyone worries, right?

THE FOUR LIES OF WORRY

To keep your adversary from blending into the scenery of your mind, you have to become adept at spotting the lies worry tells you. So let's take a look at four of worry's lies.

Lie 1: Something really bad is going to happen.

We've all been tormented by this lie. Throughout the day, as we are confronted by different situations, we too easily tilt to the negative extreme and assume something bad is going to happen. But really, only a fraction of the things we worry about come to pass. A 2019 study from Penn State showed that roughly 91 percent of the things we worry about never even happen.[1] But worry wants to convince you of what feels like the inevitability of every possible negative outcome. It tries to guarantee that your situation will end in the worst-case scenario.

There's a quote often attributed to French philosopher Michel de Montaigne, who framed this lie well when he wrote: "My life has been full of terrible misfortunes, most of which never happened."

To be clear, I'm not suggesting that bad things don't happen in life. Obviously, your story and mine affirm that they do.

---

1. Seth J. Gillihan, "How Often Do Your Worries Actually Come True?", *Psychology Today* (Sussex Publishers, July 19, 2019), https://www.psychologytoday.com/us/blog/think-act-be/201907/how-often-do-your-worries-actually-come-true.

I've lost both my parents to long-term, debilitating diseases. Pain and suffering and loss are a part of our journey on a broken planet. Jesus underscored this when He said, "In this world you will have trouble . . ." The power to deflate worry, though, is found in how Jesus finished that sentence: "but . . . I have overcome the world" (John 16:33).

So here's the new reality that allows you to combat the lie that something bad is going to happen: most of what you're spending your time worrying about won't happen. If you know and believe this ahead of time, you can cut worry off from the onset because you're now armed with the reality that "the worst" outcome statistically will not occur. The more you choose not to go down the path of worry, the better equipped you'll become.

Now, again, that's not to say that bad things won't come our way, because unfortunately we live in a broken world filled with heartache, misfortune, and loss. But what it does mean is that we don't have to overcommit our valuable time and attention toward *what-if* circumstances. If the *what if* happens, when something bad actually lands in your world, Jesus will give you what you need to overcome it.

Lie 2: The more you worry about it, the better your odds of avoiding it.

This is a tricky lie. Yes, we often have cause for concern and preparation. But the Enemy wants you to believe that if you worry or fret over a certain outcome long enough, you can keep something bad from happening.

The reality is worrying has *never* once prevented something negative from happening. Planning might. Prayer has. But worry never will.

The Enemy tells you that by worrying about a situation (or every situation) you can make your tomorrow better. Really, worry just robs you of today. Jesus implored us:

> I tell you, do not worry about your life, what you will eat or drink; or about your body, what you will wear. Is not life more than food, and the body more than clothes? Look at the birds of the air; they do not sow or reap or store away in barns, and yet your heavenly Father feeds them. Are you not much more valuable than they? . . . Therefore do not worry about tomorrow, for tomorrow will worry about itself. (Matthew 6:25–26, 34)

Your best bet for being prepared for tomorrow is to lean in and trust God with what He has put in your hands today. And when the day turns over, repeat.

One of the greatest tools to help counter the temptation to worry is recalling the faithfulness of God. In every situation, worry wants you to think, *This is the one where everything is going to go off the rails*. But the faithfulness of God tells you otherwise. It says, "Today, I will do for you what I did yesterday, and the day before, and the days before that." Faithfulness is the fuel of peace for today, while worry pushes you past today and into tomorrow.

Lie 3: I have no choice—I'm a born worrier.

As I mentioned in the introduction, I had some pretty amazing worriers in my house growing up. My dad was a champion at creating dreadful scenarios and spending his days drowning in the *what ifs* of every bad outcome. I would watch him and think, *Man, what's wrong with him?*

Abandoned by his parents as a young boy, my dad had good cause to think that around every bend in the road, another frightful, lonely night awaited him. But as a kid, I had no clue about what was going on in his mind and heart. When I was a teen, I remember him having one particularly traumatic day. Being sixteen, I was clueless about most of the weight my parents were carrying. But that night, as I went to leave our apartment and walk to a friend's house, he said, "I've just had the worst day of my life. I need everyone to just stay in the house tonight."

I turned around and went back to my room.

Not sure what's up with Dad, I thought. *But whatever that was, I'm going to just say okay and stay in tonight.*

What was going on at that moment? My dad was trying to let me know he was worried every time I left the house. And this night he couldn't bear the burden of worrying on top of what he'd been through that day.

I only fully understood this when I was older and I started having the same feelings. I realized that I, too, could easily tip toward fearing a dreadful outcome. I would naturally obsess over the question, "What's the worst thing that could happen?"

For a season, I just blamed this proclivity on my dad. *I'm a born worrier,* I thought.

But that's not my new spiritual reality. In Christ, I am born again, and "if anyone is in Christ, the new creation has come: The old has gone, the new is here!" (2 Corinthians 5:17).

Here's the new reality for you and me. We may have a genetic tendency toward worry. And, more powerfully, we may have been weaned in a worrying culture. Worry is what we saw others do. Worry is what we learned. Worry is what we are prone to repeat.

But dear friends, if you are in Christ, all those old patterns were disrupted the instant you were born again. You have a new Father in heaven. He has never worried for one second in His eternal existence. He wasn't worried yesterday. Nor is He today. He will not be worried tomorrow.

There's no doubting the fact that He is concerned for you. He manages time and the affairs of men. He loves you. You are born into a new family as a daughter or son of God through Jesus Christ. And your new family is not a worrying family. Your new family is a family of sovereign peace, knowing that God is in control. And He is enough for you in every situation.

Lie 4: I can control the outcome by worrying.

Worry wants to convince you that if you think about the situation long enough, you can control the outcome. Nothing could be further from the truth. In the end, the reality is that you, by God's grace, can control your choices and how you react to everything else. Period.

You are not God. While worry wants you to think you're in the driver's seat, worry really locks you in the trunk of the car (or "in the boot" for my English-speaking friends outside the US).

Jesus asked, "Who of you by worrying can add a single hour to your life?" Think about that for a moment. None of us can add even a second to our day. He continued, "Since you cannot do this very little thing, why do you worry about the rest?" (Luke 12:25–26).✈

Worry keeps you up at night. It convinces you that if you work at it, you can solve every problem. But in the end, peace comes by admitting that you are not God. I am not God. Therefore, I am not in charge. I am not in control. I don't run the show. I am simply a part of God's plan. Yet, I know He loves me. So I will trust and obey.

When we adopt this mindset, our prayers shift from trying to get God to give us our desired outcomes to instead saying, "God, I repent of trying to be You. Have Your will and Your way in my life."

Some could see this prayer as a cop-out. I see it as a beautiful surrender. Worry tells you that you are in charge. But who wants that job, anyway? Faith tells you the God who loves you is in charge. Your Maker is in control. You can trust Him. All His ways are good.

SPOT THE LIES AND START THE FIGHT

Those are four of the lies that worry loves to tell. They aren't the only ones, but they are some of the lies you'll encounter most. Fighting back against worry is like any other training regimen or discipline. At first, each effort feels a bit clunky and forced. If you've been sitting in worry for some time, it's likely going to be an adjustment to begin to identify the lies. They may have become more camouflaged as you've become more acquainted with their presence over time.

But it's never too late to start. And remember, through Jesus you have all the power you need to win this war on worry. Romans 8:11 says, "If the Spirit of him who raised Jesus from the dead is living in you, he who raised Christ from the dead will also give life to your mortal bodies because of his Spirit, who lives in you."

That first step might feel exhausting or awkward. It's like the first workout when you're trying to get back in shape. But stick with it and keep showing up. Keep calling out the lies that worry is speaking and keep surrendering those lies to God, replacing them with the truths of His Word. I believe that if you commit and start down this path, the Spirit will continue to empower you to fight the good fight.

Worry ultimately spends a lot of time and effort trying to get you to avoid any and all hardships that *might* come against you. The closer you stay to God and the more you call out the lies of worry, the more you'll come to realize that *avoidance* isn't the desired outcome of the Christian life. No, the goal of the life of the believer is *assurance*. Assurance is what turns a *what if* into an *even if* through the truth of *what is*. God *is* good. Loving. Kind. Mighty in power. Holy. Healer. He *is,* and because of that truth, you can have assurance no matter what comes against you.

PRAYER

Father, thank You that You are true and what You say is the truth. I am grateful for the firm foundation You provide, and I desire to anchor my life in You. I know the Enemy is working against me, but by Your power and with Your grace, help me to fight well and stand firm.

DISCUSSION AND REFLECTION QUESTIONS

1. Are there any negative thoughts that you consistently find yourself coming back to? If so, write those down below.

_____

_____

_____

_____

_____

2. Which of the four lies does worry speak to you most often?

_____

_____

_____

_____

_____

3. What are some practical tools you can use to spot the lies of worry in your day-to-day life?

_____

_____

_____

_____

_____

4. How can you invite your community to help you spot the lies of worry in your life?

_____

_____

_____

_____

_____

T W O

THE ANATOMY
OF WORRY

Years back, when NASCAR was peaking in popularity, Shelley and I attended several races with some of our six-stepsrecords artists at the invitation of NASCAR's chaplain. I'd usually do a devotional message for the pre-race chapel and pray with the drivers as they were strapping themselves into their cars before the race.

One weekend we were given the opportunity to take a few laps around the track in one of the pace cars (the cars that the drivers follow around the track at the beginning of the race) before the race started. We buckled in: me behind the driver, Shelley next to me, and singer Chris Tomlin in the front passenger seat. In a matter of seconds, we were flying around the track at well over one hundred miles per hour, at times passing within inches from the concrete wall on the inside of the track. The turns were so sharp I honestly thought the car was going to roll on its side and tumble down the embankment into the infield grass.

We were all holding on for dear life, trying to act calm and cool, but inside we were freaking out. I kept pushing an imaginary brake pedal on the floorboard and wanted to grab the wheel. The driver was talking up a storm and constantly glancing at me in the rearview mirror. *Don't you want to WATCH OUT FOR THAT WALL THAT'S FOUR INCHES FROM THE CAR?!* I was thinking.

Then I just let all that emotion and fear subside. The ride was still hair-raisingly scary, but I realized this guy driving us was a twenty-year NASCAR veteran driver, and to him, going more than a hundred and twenty miles an hour around a racetrack was like you or me casually pushing a baby stroller on a sidewalk on a summer evening. He'd spent his career driving way faster and with thirty other cars inches from his front and back bumpers and side doors.

In the end, we piled out of the car laughing and grinning about what a thrill it was. Why? Because we were not in control. A professional NASCAR driver had the steering wheel the whole time.

If you're bogged down by worry right now and feeling like you're teetering on the edge of a big tumble down the embankment in Turn 3, it's most likely because you are trying to control something (or someone) that you were not designed to control. But that's the way worry operates.

Worry always starts with a harmless seed planted in our minds. We think:

After all, shouldn't I be concerned?

It's my responsibility, so I have to care about what happens, right? Isn't it wise to prepare for all the options I might face?

Yet, if unchecked, that initial seed can morph into a more powerful negative thought, and worry can take root in our hearts.

I've found through years of conversations, reflection, and study that our worry orbits around five major themes.

1. *We worry about a dangerous outcome.* Our friend is traveling and we worry they may get in an accident. Or a child worries their parents might get a divorce. Or we worry that we'll get cancer.

2. *We worry about a threatening confrontation.* We need to have a tough conversation with a family member. We are getting a review at school or work.

3. *We worry about a shortage of resources.* We don't know if we'll ever pay off college debt. We're not sure if we'll be laid off at work. We don't know if we'll have enough time to finish the project.

4. *We worry about our ability.* Will we do well enough on the presentation? Will people like us? Will we be able to make the cut?

5. *We worry about global calamity.* Will there be a

war? What if there's a famine or the economic markets melt down? We're concerned the climate is changing, and we can't stop it.

Each of these worrisome themes takes on a slightly different shape on the outside, but underneath the surface they all share a common root—the desire for control.

————

I remember the day well. I was in middle school, with an emotion ebbing between anticipation and trepidation as we arrived at the day we were going to dissect a worm in biology class. Talk about something to worry about.

All these years later I can't remember why we were dissecting the worm, or what we learned from it, but nonetheless we were determined, as per our assignment, to open up this expired creature and see what was inside.

That's what this chapter is all about. You see, worry isn't just some hypothetical, vague concept. No, you can actually put worry on the operating table and begin to dissect the various mechanisms and internal workings of worry. In this chapter we're slicing through the outer layers of worry to expose what makes this seed of doubt and lies tick. Doing this analysis is critical for us to cultivate a peaceful heart and a confident mind. Once we get below the surface we'll discover this reality: *at the heart of worry is our need to be in control.*

If we go back to the beginning of humanity, we see that God's beautiful plan of Paradise was sabotaged by two people who made a fatal choice. Not that this was outside of God's sovereign control, but there's no denying that Adam and Eve brought consequences into an otherwise glorious circumstance. The first humans reached for the forbidden fruit and took a bold and brazen bite. Having believed the lies the Enemy put forth in questions—*Is God good? Can He be trusted?*—Adam and Eve did the one thing the Creator warned them not to do. When they held the fruit in their hands, they wanted to control their fate. They wanted to make sure they were in charge—or at least that they had as much authority and ability as the God who had formed them and given them purpose.

But, as they quickly and unfortunately discovered, it turned out God wasn't trying to keep anything from them with His command. In fact, God was seeking to protect their peaceful state. Determined to control their narrative, Adam and Eve had taken hold of the steering wheel of their destiny; and when they took control, spiritual and physical death were instantly injected into humankind's story.

Many of us are familiar with the story, but I pray today that this familiarity would not cloud our eyes from seeing the radical truths presented in these chapters of Scripture. It's not hard to believe that the Enemy comes against us and is bold enough to tempt us, even after we put our faith in Jesus. But friends, it should be shocking to us that the Enemy's tactics of worry and doubt worked in Paradise! That's how bold and cunning he is. It's one thing to try to make someone doubt God's goodness in the midst of the pain and death we face on a broken planet. But how do you get someone who lives in Paradise to fall for a lie? Crazy, right? Yet, we know that the devil succeeded in a perfect setting, so you should be convinced he'll be bold enough to come after you.

The heart of his plan will be a two-pronged attack.

First, he'll attempt to get you to doubt God's character and motives.

Second, he will try to convince you that life will be better when you are in control—when you take matters into your own hands.

The way we deflect both attacks is through the cross of Christ. That might feel like a bit of a left turn, but stay with me.

To the first question of God's character and motives, we can never forget that in a real moment in history, Jesus Christ gave His life by enduring death on a Roman cross. Jesus laid down His life for us so we could be forgiven and have eternal life. There is no greater proof of God's character and motives than this: "Greater love has no one than this: to lay down one's life for one's friends" (John 15:13). When we look back at the cross, we see that there's no doubting the fact that God is good and that He can be trusted.

For the second lie, that our lives will be better when we are in control, I bring you to the cross again. The scene on the day Jesus was crucified was mayhem. It was brutal injustice. Humankind's pride was on full display. Guilt and despair were in the air. People were trying to seize control of the religious and political climates. Rulers were protecting their power. The religious elite were guarding their system. Why? Because sin was now a part of the human story. Adam and Eve took matters into their own hands and flexed their will over God's plan. And how did that go? It ended up with humankind having a deadly sinful nature we couldn't cure, and the innocent Son of God being nailed to a cross so He could set right what had been broken and restore us to the Creator who is and always has been fully in control.

So what does this redemption truth have to do with worry?

Sin brought death. When we lived under the banner of death, we felt compelled to try to control every outcome, because if we didn't, who would? Our need for control was rooted in fear, and it fueled our anxiety (Romans 8:15). We were fed the lie that we could become masters of our own fate. All the while, our end destination was determined: death.

Think of it this way: we are trying to control life that

inevitably ends in death. Yet God has stepped into the story with stunning grace and upended the power of death (1 Corinthians 15:26–28). It was His plan from the beginning of time (Acts 4:26–28). Jesus' resurrection puts the brakes on our need for control because we can fully trust that the One who overcame death, hell, and the grave loves us and gives His victorious life to us through Jesus Christ. He promises to care for us. Guide us. Protect us.

One of the most sobering descriptions of the victory of Jesus is found in Isaiah 53:4–5. Here we read that "Surely [Jesus] took up our pain and bore our suffering, yet we considered him punished by God, stricken by him, and afflicted. But he was pierced for our transgressions, he was crushed for our iniquities; the punishment that brought us peace was on him, and by his wounds we are healed."

Jesus can carry what is worrying you because He has already carried what was meant to kill you. He has already carried your sorrows and buried them in His grave.

So if at the heart of worry is a desire for control, how do you change? How do you win the battle on worry and find peace, especially when the world around you seems out of control? You find peace by surrendering your need for control to the One who is actually in control.

If someone else in that car had taken the wheel while we were whizzing around that NASCAR track, I would have been shouting, "Pull this baby over! I'm getting out now!" But I knew the person in control was legitimately good at being in control.

Scripture says: "Before the mountains were born or you brought forth the whole world, from everlasting to everlasting you are God" (Psalm 90:2). In Isaiah 46 God's Word reminds us of just how in control God is:

I am God, and there is no other; I am God, and there is none like me. I make known the end from the beginning, from ancient times, what is still to come. I say, 'My purpose will stand, and I will do all that I please.' (vv. 9–10)

God has been running the universe for a long, long time. That means you can let go.

Surrender your need to be in charge. Trust that His

heart for you is good. Place in His hands whatever is causing you to worry right now. Believe God is good at being in control.

Now, I know what you're thinking. You're probably reading this and saying, "Louie, am I really not supposed to control *anything*? I thought there was some benefit to being prepared and concerned."

And you'd be right. There is a benefit to being concerned or preparing for something. But the answer lies in separating concern or preparation from worry, because as we'll find out in the next chapter, they are two very different things.

PRAYER

Father, I surrender my need for control to You. I humble myself under Your kind and righteous hand, believing and trusting that You are able to work all things out in ways that glorify You and that bring me the fruit of the Spirit. I release my heavy burden of needing to be in charge, and I take the freedom Your Son accomplished for me.

DISCUSSION AND REFLECTION QUESTIONS

1. What are you trying to control right now? What do you need to relinquish to God?

_____

_____

_____

_____

_____

2. Write out what is currently worrying you. Then, write out a corresponding truth about the character of God for each concern. How can you frequently remind yourself of these truths of God's character?

_____

_____

_____

_____

_____

3. When you think about the cross of Jesus, what comes
   to your mind or stirs in your heart?

_____

_____

_____

_____

_____

4. Read Isaiah 46 and write out four truths about the
   nature and character of God.

_____

_____

_____

_____

_____

THREE

EMBRACING CONCERN, REJECTING WORRY

I am fully convinced that I am married to the best human being on the planet. Every chance I get, I'm telling people about how amazing Shelley is. She's whip-smart, super talented, humble, wise, loving, gentle, and all-around fun. She's beautiful both inside and out, and she has changed my life in more ways than I can possibly outline here.

We've been married now for thirty-six years, and over that time, I've come to appreciate many things about Shelley. But near the top on that list is the fact that she is an A-to-Z girl.

Here's what I mean by that.

People I lead and people who work for me know that I'm an A-to-B guy. I like big vision. I feel like it's one of the things that God has uniquely gifted me for. I love to seek the huge endeavor, something that hasn't been done by someone in quite that way before. But as soon as a new venture is getting traction and getting off the ground, I start to lose interest and move on. I helped get us from point A to point B (and, at times, a lot farther), but for me there are more ideas to be had, more visions to dream for.

That's what I mean when I say I'm an A-to-B guy. So what do you think that means when I say that Shelley is an A-to-Z girl? It means that she is the planner, the strategist, and the executor of our duo. She takes an idea and carries it to completion, through every hoop and over every hurdle. She gets things done, and she doesn't stop until things are finished—and finished well. I've usually moved on to seven new things while Shelley is actually making good on every plan we started.

I don't know which of these two personalities you gravitate toward, but I do know that worry can infiltrate either.

We learned in the previous chapter about the anatomy of worry and how the different themes of worry are connected by the same thread: control. And while we determined that our ability to control our lives is an illusion, we still need to address the question of how we can reject control and fear while still accounting for planning, preparation, and concern. Because here's the curveball: God calls you to steward what you have in your hands. He gives you decision-making authority over what He has entrusted to you.

In Matthew 25 Jesus told a parable that dealt with a master who went away for an extended period. Before he went away, he gave a considerable amount of money to three of his servants. To the first servant, Scripture says the master gave five talents. Don't be confused by the small number—a talent was equivalent to twenty years of wages for a laborer.[1] To put that in context, the master gave his servant roughly the same amount of money as if he would have labored six days a week for a hundred years!

---

1. *Lexham Bible Dictionary*, s.v. "talent," accessed May 2, 2022, https://biblia.com/factbook/Talent.

To the second servant, the master gave two talents, and to the last servant, the master gave one talent. Anyway, you may know how the story goes. The master left, and the servants managed the money. The first two invested it and leveraged it, likely in the cattle or agrarian industries of the day. But the third servant? He decided to follow a different path. Afraid of his master and the possibility of losing the money, he buried it. Better safe and in the ground than at risk and in the open.

The master returned and praised the servants who invested well. The master said that they were "good and faithful" (Matthew 25:21). They made a plan, prepared, and were concerned for the welfare of the work assigned to them. The master rewarded them by giving them even more than they were originally entrusted with.

What do we learn here? Planning isn't a bad thing. In fact, being a good steward with our time and resources is one of the ways we can glorify God in this world. Ephesians 5:15–16 says to "be very careful, then, how you live—not as unwise but as wise, making the most of every opportunity, because the days are evil."

LEARNING TO PLAN WITHOUT PRACTICING WORRY

So how do we do that? How do we plan and show concern without tipping over into worry? Well, first we need to define some terms to make sure we're all on the same page.

Let's look at how we define *planning*.

Planning is a constructive and tangible process where steps and actions are linked together for future outcomes. When we are planning well, variables are considered and countered, and best practices rise to the top and are acted on.

While planning, contingencies are always in place for unexpected events or delays. But these contingency plans do not impede our ability to move toward the next step with confidence.

In other words, planning is about leveraging your gifts and resources around what is in your hand at this moment, and moving it forward, step by step.

Now let's look at *worry*.

If planning is a constructive and tangible process, worry is the projection of an endless string of *what-if* scenarios that absorbs all present effort (what you could be doing with what is currently in your hands). This string of *what ifs* often brings fear and paralysis that keeps us from our next steps.

Planning focuses on the present and on what is in your hands, while occasionally looking ahead to factor in what is to come. Worry fixates on the future, while occasionally circling back to "work" on what is currently in front of you.

Do you see the difference?

The third servant in the story of the talents got paralyzed by the *what ifs*. *What if I lose the money? What if I'm not capable? What if the other servants outearn me? What if I get sick or injured? What if something big happens to all the livestock in my town and I'm caught up in financial ruin? What if I fail? What if I lose my job? My family? My home?*

Scripture actually says he was "afraid" (Matthew 25:25). Isn't it interesting that the result of getting caught in the web of *what ifs* is fear? Remember how I mentioned that worry is rooted in fear? In this parable we see Jesus showing us that connection.

While the first two servants were concerned and

practiced good planning, this servant got stuck in a stream of worry. And once he got into the stream, he eventually got stuck in the whirlpool of self-doubt.

In our fast-paced, multitasking world, it can be easy, even natural, to think seven steps ahead. To always be projecting far-out scenarios and mental models of what might happen. If we spend too much time hanging around the *what ifs*, the toxicity of worry begins to poison our hearts and minds.

It's not wrong to admit that the occasional *what if* can be helpful. Like we covered earlier, every so often when you're building a plan, you need to look ahead. But you can't live there. You can't fixate so much on the ideas of tomorrow that you cease living in the realities of today. Not only is it detrimental to your spiritual health, but psychology and sociology have proven that it's actually a large waste of time and effort. As we mentioned earlier in this book, research actually shows us that most of the *what ifs* that we project and dwell on don't ever happen.

According to *Psychology Today*, in a small study done at Penn State University, scientists and doctors set out to expose a group of volunteers to as many possible stress-points as was feasible in a ten-day window. Then they observed if those stress-points, or *what ifs*, actually came to pass.

After thirty days of observation, the team conducting the study noted that 91 percent of worries did not materialize. Yes, 91 percent![2]

What does this mean for us? It means that what's most important is what is in our hands right now—what we are tangibly carrying. Yes, the future is important, and wise preparation will almost certainly be beneficial, but if 91 percent of future worries never come to pass, we need to get out of the stream of worry and *what ifs* and get back on to the path of making the most of what God has assigned to us today.

PRACTICAL STEPS TO PLAN WELL

We've spent some time looking at Scripture and science. Now let's downshift and get practical for a moment. Because

---

2. Seth J. Gillihan, PhD, "How Often Do Your Worries Actually Come True?", *Psychology Today,* July 29, 2019, https://www.psychologytoday.com/us/blog /think-act-be/201907/how-often-do-your-worries-actually-come-true.

here's the reality about planning: you can talk about it all you want, but eventually you need to cross that line from theoretical to practical. So how can you plan without tipping over into worry? Here are a few steps.

Do what is in your hands to do today. (And, by the way, crush it!) Do your absolute best work, not for men but for the Lord (Colossians 3:23). The servants who invested the money for their master did a great job. They doubled their deposit!

Don't pick up any not-yet-realized challenges until necessary. Jesus said that today has enough trouble of its own (Matthew 6:34), so don't add to tomorrow's challenges ahead of time.

Recognize that the Master is returning and stay prepared. We've been entrusted with something valuable—the King's things (Luke 12:42–43). If that's the case, we should be grateful, humbled, and ready for His return.

Planning well and steering clear from worry means that

we embrace the mentality of *I'll cross that bridge when I get to it.* Now, that doesn't necessarily mean we get to totally stop thinking about the bridge or even that we get to quit working to prepare for some of the necessary details of crossing the bridge.

But it does mean we don't allow ourselves to fall into the trap of worrying about if the bridge might have collapsed before we even get to it.

If you take one more look at the parable of the talents, you may think, *I'm all in on focusing on what has been placed in my hands. But Louie, what if what's in my hands is too much for me to carry?*

This is a valid question, and it's one that Jesus answered in a few simple words. In Matthew 25:15 Jesus said, "To one he gave five talents, to another two, and to another one, to each according to his own ability" (NKJV).

God puts things into your hands according to your ability and His power to work in and through you. If He's entrusted it to you, you can carry it. If He's calling you to it, He will be faithful and help you through it. If He's placed it in your hands, you don't need to worry about where it will end up. You just need to prepare, plan, and stay ready—because the King will come back for the King's things.

PRAYER

Father, I bring to You the things I am concerned about. Help me make wise choices to bring about the best outcomes in every situation. Give me the grace to place what I cannot control into Your hands with confidence and peace.

DISCUSSION AND REFLECTION QUESTIONS

1. What has God placed in your hands today? Take some time to thank God for what He has graciously given to you.

_____

_____

_____

_____

_____

2. Identify a time in your life when your planning
   turned into worry. Looking back, was there a tipping
   point you can recognize now?

_____

_____

_____

_____

_____

3. Read James 4:13–17. How can you cultivate a spirit of
   "if it is the Lord's will" (v. 15)?

_____

_____

_____

_____

_____

4. If you were to stop overthinking your plans, what
   would that free you up to do more of today?

_____

_____

_____

_____

_____

FOUR

INVITING GOD INTO
YOUR WORRY

We're only a few chapters in, but we have covered a lot of
ground together. I'm hopeful that you are beginning to see
tangible progress in your war on worry. By doing some of
the background work of identifying *who* worry is (a liar) and
what worry is made of (its anatomy—rooted in fear), we can
know our Enemy and his tactics. And knowing our Enemy
is essential to being able to fight well.

In *The Art of War,* famous strategist Sun Tzu said, "If
you know the enemy and know yourself, you need not fear
the result of a hundred battles. If you know yourself but
not the enemy, for every victory gained you will also suffer

a defeat. If you know neither the enemy nor yourself, you will succumb in every battle."[1]

As we continue this journey to become more equipped to win the war on worry, we know our Enemy: his sole purpose is to take us down and steal our joy (John 10:10). That's why we're fighting back. We also need to know ourselves; and most importantly, we need to know our God. Because here's the reality: if we don't know God, we won't be able or willing to invite Him into our worry.

That's a big problem, because the act of inviting God into our worry is one of the most crucial strategies of winning this war.

GOING ON THE OFFENSIVE

It's not enough to call worry out or to break it down and study it. If we want to win this battle, we need to strap on our armor and get ready to go on the offensive. And you

---

1. Sun Tzu, *The Art of War,* trans. Lionel Giles (Mineola, NY: Dover, 2002), 51.

want to know our first move of attack? To surrender our concerns to God in prayer.

Paul said it this way: "Don't worry about anything; instead, pray about everything. Tell God what you need, and thank him for all he has done" (Philippians 4:6 NLT).

You may hear that and say, "Telling me not to worry is like telling snow not to melt in the summer heat." I hear you, and I admit that I've felt that way at times in my life. I still occasionally find myself feeling burdened by the weight of worry.

But notice that Paul wasn't just saying "don't worry." He was giving you an additional offensive step to take. He was encouraging you to invite God into your worry by telling Him everything that's concerning you.

The word *worry* in this verse means "to rip into pieces."[2] It's the same for the word *anxiety* in Scripture. Anxiety and worry tear our minds and hearts apart. That's why we have the phrase, "I was worried to pieces." Worry turns our *peace* into *pieces*. But here's the good news: God wants us to bring every little piece to Him. That's the first step in how God brings us peace.

---

2. "Merimnaó," Strong's Greek: 3309. μεριμνάω (merimnaó)—to be anxious, to care for, accessed May 9, 2022, https://biblehub.com/greek/3309.htm.

Back in Paradise when Adam and Eve sinned, they immediately felt guilty and hid from God. That's our natural response when we know we have missed the mark and fallen short of His glory. We run *from* God when we need to be running *to* Him.

If you're stuck in the mire of worry and think there's no way out, don't try to fix it on your own. If you're ashamed that you can't do better and you feel like a failure, don't hide from God. Instead, call out to Him. Invite Him into the web of anxiety and turn the negative energy of worry into the positive activity of prayer. Tell God what you need and thank Him for all He's done for you.

Now God is in the middle of the worry with you. And the great news is that He's never worried about anything.

So how do we tap into that kind of confidence?

ABIDING IN THE EVERLASTING VINE

We counter anxiety by abiding. And what does it mean to abide? To remain. To dwell. To stay in a constant posture of surrender and dependency, not on your own strength and your own power but on the character and nature of God.

Let's look at John 15:5. In this verse Jesus said, "I am the vine; you are the branches. Those who remain in me, and I in them, will produce much fruit. For apart from me you can do nothing" (NLT).

I love this verse because I think it's full of good news. First, we see right off the bat what our role is in this whole story. We are the branches. Jesus is the Vine. That means that He's the source of life. Of nutrients—of richness and vitality. He is our Source. We are the receivers.

As branches, our job is to remain. We are to stay connected to the Vine; and when we do, we bear much fruit.

What kind of fruit do we bear? Paul talked about it in Galatians 5 when he said, "The fruit of the Spirit is love, joy, peace, patience, kindness, goodness, faithfulness, gentleness, and self-control" (22–23 ESV).

Do you see *worry* in that list? Do you see *fear*, or *control*, or *anxiety*? No! When we invite God into our worry, we surrender or offboard our need for control and we onboard His call to dwell and abide in Him. And the next thing we know, we're bearing fruit. We're blossoming with patience, love, and peace.

But let's get even more practical.

For most of us, the primary reason we fall short on abiding and dwelling with God isn't because we're not spiritual enough or because we don't understand the concept. Most of us could quote some version of the fruit of the Spirit and would likely know Paul's command not to be anxious about anything.

Here's our greatest opponent in this war: we're easily distracted.

ABIDING VS. DIVIDING

There are many things that steal our attention and *divide* our focus from the call to *abide* and dwell with God. We could look at a dozen different distractions and make a battle plan against each, but for now, we'll just focus on one: our screens.

The average person spends around three hours a day looking at their smartphone (and a good percentage of people spend even more time).[3] In fact, we are so easily distracted by our screens that we go to touch our phones and other devices more than 2,600 times a day.[4]

That's a lot. Especially when you compare it to the five to ten minutes a day we *might* spend in devotion and solitude with the God of the universe.

Now I'm not here to place blame or throw stones. I use my phone just like the next person. But I am trying to get a point across.

Instead of meditating with the One who created us, we're medicating ourselves with hits of dopamine and blasts of simulated joy. We've taken a step away from solitude and surrender and instead moved toward the storm. We're saying that we want still water, but all the while we continue to row right toward the hurricane.

The thing with abiding is that it takes time. Just as it's hard to pour water into a shaky cup, it's difficult for the

3. Abral Al-Heeti, "We'll Spend Nearly a Decade of Our Lives Staring at Our Phones, Study Says," CNET, November 12, 2020, https://www.cnet.com/tech/mobile/well-spend-nearly-a-decade-of-our-lives-staring-at-our-phones-study-says/.
4. Julia Naftulin, "Here's How Many Times We Touch Our Phones Every Day," *Business Insider*, July 13, 2016, https://www.businessinsider.com/dscout-research-people-touch-cell-phones-2617-times-a-day-2016-7.

peace of God to flow into a heart that's in constant motion. When we quiet ourselves and sit before Him—really sit and create space to surrender our fears, our anxieties, our burdens to Him—then we abide. Then we get connected to the Vine of life, and up from our hearts springs peace, kindness, and self-control.

For some of us, slowing down can begin with a step as simple as changing the way we breathe.

The process of inhaling and exhaling is near mindless. It's a function we need to survive, but it is so commonplace that we rarely think about it in our day-to-day. What if we took this one biological function and used it as a spark to move us back toward abiding in the Vine? Here's how.

We start by breathing out the lies that cause us to feel anxious or stressed. It might sound like this: breathe out, "I'm alone." We expel that lie away from our minds. But that's just the first part. Next, we need to fill that space with something good, something true. As we breathe in, we claim a promise of God. It could sound like this: breathe in, "God is with me."

See how that works? Let's look at a few more examples.

Breathe out, "I'm abandoned." Breathe in, "God is
 in me."
Breathe out, "My enemies are against me." Breathe in,
 "God is for me."
Breathe out, "I am weak." Breathe in, "God is bigger
 than me."
Breathe out, "I am lacking." Breathe in, "God is
 enough for me."
Breathe out, "I am forgotten." Breathe in, "God is
 faithful to me."

What if you took a few minutes, put your phone in the
other room, and slowed yourself down to focus on your
breathing? What would that change in your life? What kind
of fruit do you think you'd start noticing as you learn to
abide in the vine?

Here's the last thing I'll say on what it means to invite
God into our worry: when we spend time with Jesus, when
we read His Word and meditate on His truth and His life,
we begin to unlock something in our souls.

We're trained to identify problems and to come up with

fixes that will get us through, get us over, or get us around the issue. But that's not the answer to our war on worry.

When it comes to our war, we don't need a solution. We need a Savior. And thankfully, we have one. His name is Jesus. He's not just a nice guy floating through the pages of history. Jesus is an undisputed champion, death defeater, cosmos Creator, matchless light that sets darkness to flight.

And as we'll see in the next chapter, His perfect love changes everything.

PRAYER

Father, thank You that You are bigger than we think You are. Thank You that even though You created the cosmos, You hear us when we pray, and therefore You listen as we invite You into our hearts and into our worry. Help us breathe in Your promises and breathe out Your hope, Your goodness, Your victory. We are Your children, and through You, we will be victorious in this war.

DISCUSSION AND
REFLECTION QUESTIONS

1. Take two minutes, shut down your phone, sit in the quiet, and focus on your breathing. Breathe in deeply through your nose and out through your mouth. Make a note of how you feel.

_____

_____

_____

_____

_____

2. Galatians 5 compares the fruit of the flesh with the fruit of the Spirit. Read over those Scriptures and reflect. Which of those fruit are currently most evident in your life?

_____

_____

_____

_____

_____

3. God wants to hear about what concerns you. What holds you back from going to God with the big and small things that weigh you down?

_____

_____

_____

_____

_____

4. The Scriptures often describe God as a place of refuge. What does *refuge* mean, and why would it be beneficial for you to have a strong and sturdy refuge to run to?

_____

_____

_____

_____

_____

FIVE

THE POWER OF PERFECT LOVE

We don't invite God into our worry just because we want His solution or His quick fix. Worry has never been overcome and defeated with a little spiritual duct tape. Instead, when we invite God into our worry, we begin to realize that more than any solution, He wants to give us a Savior. He wants to invite us into an intimate and personal relationship with His Son. Why? Because God knows what we truly need.

The counteragent for worry isn't control. It's faith

rooted in love. And this is the best possible news you or I could hope for—because our God is the only source of perfect love, and you're on His radar.

I moved to Texas after graduating from college to go to seminary. I was dating Shelley at the time and she was wrapping up her undergrad degree at Baylor University. We were in a long-distance relationship, but this was different from what likely comes to mind when you read those words now. This was before mobile phones or video calling or social media. Needless to say, we had to come up with creative ways to show that we cared about each other, which often meant me spending long hours in the car driving to see her.

I remember one particular time when it had been a while since we'd last been in the same space. I was missing Shelley, so after studying in the library one night, I got in my car and just started driving. I didn't have a plan, and I wasn't exactly sure how it was all going to play out. I just knew that I wanted to see her and I wanted her to know how much she meant to me.

It was late at night by the time I got to campus. I sat two

cans of Hawaiian Punch (our favorite drink at the time) on the counter outside the RA's office in her dorm and asked her to call up to Shelley's room and tell her someone had left something at the desk for her. Then I hid behind a wall in the lobby so I could covertly watch her reaction. When she came down and saw the drinks, she knew I was there and immediately started looking around for me. Shelley was studying for an exam the next morning so we literally spent fifteen minutes hanging out on the steps of her dorm, and then I had to leave. But it was worth it!

As I drove off, I started thinking about all the "cute" Baylor boys who were probably trying to impress my girl, so I decided to make a statement. I drove a few blocks down to the H-E-B grocery store and reached in my wallet to scrounge up enough cash to buy a poster board, some markers, plastic wrap, and a few nails.

Supplies in hand, I drove back toward her dorm. I knew from previous visits where her room was in the building and that it overlooked the courtyard below. I found a tree that I thought was in a direct sight line from her window.

All she had to do was open her blinds in the morning

and she'd be staring straight at this tree. I made sure my poster was facing her second-floor window and would survive the drizzle that was steadily falling.

Once I had my plan, I got to work. Several hours later a huge red heart filled the poster that was now nailed to the tree and was positioned for the wake-up call I would give Shelley the next morning. Happy with my plan, I got in my car and proceeded to drive all the way back home.

Why did I do that? Because I was hopelessly in love with this girl? Yes. But there's an even more important reason I made that drive and nailed that sign on the tree. You see, I loved Shelley, but I wanted her to *know* that I loved her without a shadow of a doubt. And I wanted her to know the next morning that all she had to do was sit up and crack the blinds to see the "I love you" I had left for her.

If we understand how to express our love, how much more does God know and choose to express His love for us? If, with our limited knowledge, we can still grasp how important love is, how much more will God seek to make His love known?

GOD'S GREAT LOVE FOR YOU

Do you realize God has left a stunningly powerful message of love for you? He hung the greatest "I love you" of all time on a tree at Calvary through the death of His Son. You can see His message from wherever you are today if you just turn and look toward the cross.

In Jeremiah 31 we find these words: "The LORD appeared to us in the past, saying: 'I have loved you with an everlasting love; I have drawn you with unfailing kindness'" (v. 3).

God loves us. Perfectly. I know that sounds simplistic, as it echoes the anthem we likely grew up singing in our church nursery, "Jesus loves me, this I know, for the Bible tells me so." But even though this sounds simple, so many of us still wrestle with how to embrace this foundational, life-shaping, worry-conquering truth.

Jesus loves you.

His love for you does not ebb and flow based on your position or performance. He is not carefully dialing in and calibrating His love for you based on your potential or what you may one day accomplish for the kingdom of God. He is not reserving some of His love for when you prove your dedication and commitment for His mission.

He has never loved you more because of your good deeds, nor has He ever loved you less because of the sinful acts you have committed. He *is* love. His love is unchanging. It is the same yesterday, today, and tomorrow. It's unending and eternal. His love was full before there was a single speck of dust that He would later use to fashion you and me. His love is in every minute and every moment of today, and His love will be in the future. Permanently. His love will fill heaven and be the everlasting source of joy, pleasure, and praise when there is no more measurement of hours, days, or years— when time ceases to exist and all we have is all of Him.

His love is undefeatable and unfailing. It has never lost an inch of ground, never taken a step back in shock or surprise. It has never turned away from you, never given up on you, never stopped pursuing you.

His love is perfect.

And when we get that perfect love in our vision, locked into the center of the eyes of our heart as Paul said in Ephesians 1:18, we see that love and embrace that truth. In

His love we have the only weapon we'll ever need to extinguish and eradicate worry from our lives.

WHAT'S YOUR OPERATING SYSTEM?

Maybe you're the kind of person who learns from practical examples, so let me break it down for you. We've become more familiar in recent years with the term *operating system*. It's the software that empowers our phones, computers, tablets, and so forth. It feels like every few months, major technology companies are coming out with new and improved operating systems. Faster. Smarter. Sleeker. More user friendly. The works.

We may find an operating system to be common in our technology, but the truth is, you and I have our own operating systems as well. We have a hardware (our bodies) and a software (our minds and spirits). When it comes to winning the war on worry by recognizing the power of perfect love, we need to take a step back and ask ourselves, what operating system are we using?

This is the breakdown of where most of our worry comes from:

Fear → Control → Worry

We entertain feelings of fear, often stemming from questions starting with, *"What if?"* Think back to chapter 1: *What if I get sick? What if I don't measure up? What if I lose a loved one or my job or my house? What if she walks away from the marriage? What if people found out just how broken I am?*

Our fear leads us to try to control. To try to stand up and straighten up. To take the necessary actions to avoid negative outcomes. But our shoulders were never meant to carry the weight of being in full control. So, as we realize that control is actually quicksand pulling us even farther under, we begin to worry.

That's the operating system for many people on earth. Fear spawns the need for control, which gives birth to worry. And from worry comes a whole host of unhealthy practices and compromises.

If that's the formula for how the world operates, what about how we as children of God should operate? It goes like this:

Love → Surrender → Trust

When we invite God into our worry and dwell in an abiding relationship with Jesus, our operating system shifts. Instead of fear being the motivator for our lives, we start with love.

That's what Scripture means when it says in 1 John 4:18–19: "There is no fear in love. But perfect love drives out fear, because fear has to do with punishment. The one who fears is not made perfect in love. We love because he first loved us."

Did you catch that? When we experience and internalize the perfect love of God, there is no room for fear. It's not a joint partnership or a mixed bag. Perfect love drives out fear. And once fear is gone, we no longer have the pressing need for control. Instead, we can be free to fully surrender and submit to the perfect love of God because we trust that His love is not only His best offering, it's what's best for us! And without that thread of control, there is nothing to worry about.

We find ourselves with the freedom to join in the radical expression of the apostle Paul in Romans 8:31, when he shouted, "If God is for us, who can be against us?" In the next verse Paul went on to give his reasoning behind such a bold statement: "He who did not spare his own Son, but gave him up for us all—how will he not also, along with him, graciously give us all things?" (v. 32).

Do you see the connection? Worry has no place in our hearts because God loved us so much that He already sent His Son for us. He didn't spare Jesus but instead sent Him to show us how perfectly and how much He loves us.

If God was willing to do that, how will He not also help us overcome every fear and source of worry in our lives? It would be like someone being willing to give you their house but then refusing to give you a one-dollar bill. Except even that analogy falls short a thousand times over.

Can God grant you peace? He didn't spare Jesus, so yes. Why wouldn't He also give peace? Can He give you comfort? Assurance? Freedom? Joy? Hope? Yes, yes, yes, yes, and yes. Do you see that logical reality? If God already gave you His *best*, He has no reason to withhold the *rest* from you.

I want to point out one last thing about that text in Romans 8:32. It ends with the phrase *all things*. Paul wrote,

"How will he not also, along with him, graciously give us all things?" The term for *all things* in Greek is *pas*. It means "each, every, any, all, the whole."[1] In other words, *everything*. It's a common word throughout the New Testament, but Paul used it specifically here in Romans 8:32 as a reference phrase back to an earlier verse: Romans 8:28. You may not know it from memory, but you've likely heard it quoted before: "We know that in *all things* God works for the good of those who love him, who have been called according to his purpose" (emphasis added).

Do you see that correlation? God, along with Jesus, loves you so much that He is willing to give you all things. And all those things that He is giving you, He is committed to working out for your good.

That word *good* is a bit tricky because it doesn't always mean positive external circumstances. Remember: we know people still walk through very real and very difficult circumstances. We live on a broken planet, with an actual and vicious Enemy. But that word *good* means that you're

---

1. *Strong's Concordance*, G3956, s.v. "pas," https://bible.knowing-jesus.com/strongs /G3956.

going to win in the end. When the final curtain falls, when the last bell is rung, and the time ticks down to zero, you know what you can expect?

Goodness.

Victory.

Joy.

God is committed to working *all things* out for the good of those who love Him. He's proven it by not sparing His only Son but sending Him. And through Jesus' blood, you and I can use a new operating system to replace fear and grow in love.

We can't finish this chapter without taking a moment to ask the biggest question you can ever ask: Do you believe God loves you?

Not just that He likes you when you are doing good things for Him. Not that He tolerates you even though you occasionally slip up from being holy. But that He loves you, and that nothing—absolutely and unequivocally nothing—can separate you from that love?

If you believe that and hold it in your heart and mind, you have the greatest and only weapon you will ever need to put a dagger through the heart of worry.

PRAYER

Father, I'm humbled and in awe of the great power of Your love. You have done what I could never do, so I worship You because You deserve every ounce of my affection. Bury the seeds of Your love deep within my heart and draw out the resulting fruit, as Your Spirit moves me to see and savor You more.

DISCUSSION AND REFLECTION QUESTIONS

1. Recall the last time you demonstrated your love for someone else. How did that make you feel, and what does that tell you about how God loves you?

_____

_____

_____

_____

_____

2. Fear → Control → Worry or Love → Surrender → Trust. What operating system do you find yourself falling back on more often than others? What circumstances trigger you toward one operating system or the other?

_____

_____

_____

_____

_____

3. What would change in your life if you more richly understood how much God loves you?

_____

_____

_____

_____

_____

4. Read 1 John 4. What truths do you see in this
    chapter that relate to the love of God? How can you
    internalize one or two of those truths today?

_____

_____

_____

_____

_____

SIX

PUTTING A DAGGER IN THE HEART OF WORRY

I want to pause briefly and congratulate you on getting to this point. One of the reasons worry tends to linger in so many of our lives is because of our casual acceptance of the status quo. Worry far too often blends into our background as just another thing that "happens" to us. Like being hungry. Or feeling sleepy. Worry worms its way into our psyches as just something else we're bound or destined to feel.

But no more. You've walked this far, and now it's time to finish what you started. You've done the due diligence of dragging the idea of worry out of the shadows and into the light. We've dissected where worry comes from and why it tends to latch onto our lives. We know the counteragent, and we've picked up the needed weapons to fight this war. Now it's time to put a dagger in the heart of worry once and for all. Are you with me?

In the previous chapter we looked at how the perfect love of God drives out fear and leads us to surrender our idea of control, which then leads us to worship rather than worry. The more we discover about the love of God, the more we're wanting and willing to surrender, and the more worship we give to Him.

The amazing part of this reality is the more we delight in God, the more we discover that He delights in us. While He is fully content in and of Himself, and while He doesn't need anything, He chooses to lavish us with His love and to rejoice over us.

That's what Zephaniah 3:17 says: "The LORD your God is with you, the Mighty Warrior who saves. He will take great delight in you; in his love he will no longer rebuke you, but will rejoice over you with singing."

God takes great delight in you. He quiets all forms of worry and anxiety with His perfect love. And just in case you are ever tempted to listen to the sound of the world and be pulled back into fear, God says that He rejoices over you with singing. His voice is all you need. His delight is your life. His love is your victory.

So with this truth in hand, how do we go about winning the war on worry? We take back the battleground of our minds. We tear down the house that worry built, and we set out to build a new and peace-filled home on the most stable rock and foundation—the person and work of Jesus.

It might be a brick-by-brick process, but I am confident that we can renew our minds and root out worry for good.

IT'S TIME FOR A HOME RENOVATION

Let's start by demolishing the house at 1274 Worry Avenue, that mindset of worry that has gripped you in fear for as long as you can remember. This house has to come down!

And the wrecking ball that turns this house of lies into a pile of rubble is the power of the name of Jesus.

Paul wrote: "The weapons we fight with are not the weapons of the world. On the contrary, they have divine power to demolish strongholds. We demolish arguments and every pretension that sets itself up against the knowledge of God, and we take captive every thought to make it obedient to Christ" (2 Corinthians 10:4–5).

I expand on this in greater detail in my book *Don't Give the Enemy a Seat at Your Table*, but in short, you have the power through Christ to identify and bind the power of every lie that comes into your mind. You can take captive *every thought*! When you commit to this and put it into practice, you begin tearing down the house that worry built, brick by brick and thought by thought.

Demolition can be fun, but don't expect it to be a walk in the park. And don't expect the Enemy to just roll over and let you dismantle the house he's worked to build in your heart and mind without a fight. Some of you know exactly what I'm talking about. Whenever you set out to make a change, to start tearing down bricks and demolishing strongholds, the

Enemy seems to rise up and attack with even more vengeance. Even the apostle Paul felt this reality, as we read in Romans 7.

But Scripture doesn't leave us to process this alone. In fact, it gives us great comfort and confidence that not only do we have mighty and eternal weapons to overcome the darkness, but as the prophet Isaiah said, "no weapon forged against you will prevail" (Isaiah 54:17). You have all you need, offensively *and* defensively, to start this process of demolishing the house that worry built.

But let's be clear about one thing: We're not just aiming for a scrap heap where the old house of worry once stood. The goal is a new house—a new way of thinking.

We've already looked at Philippians 4:6 in an earlier chapter, yet this entire section of Scripture is a capstone passage describing the battle plan against worry. I want to park us in verse 8 of that chapter, because it's here that we see how to practically put a dagger through the heart of worry.

Here's what verse 8 says:

Finally, brothers and sisters, whatever is true, whatever is noble, whatever is right, whatever is pure, whatever is

lovely, whatever is admirable—if anything is excellent
or praiseworthy—think about such things.

That's the answer. Did you catch it? How do we drive
a dagger through the heart of worry? We think about different things than the things that are causing us to worry.

At this point, you're probably thinking, *Come on. It can't
be that easy.* And in some ways, you're right. We've all been
in a place where we try to sit still for a few moments and
our thoughts start running wild, pinging from one problem
to the next. Controlling and then changing what you think
about isn't easy. But that doesn't mean that the solution can't
be this simple. For most of our dealings with worry, it really
does boil down to us changing the way we think.

The Roman philosopher and orator Lucius Seneca once
said, "There are more things . . . likely to frighten us than
there are to crush us; we suffer more often in our imagina-
tion than in reality."[1]

You see, worry is born from fear and the attempt for

---

1. Lucius Seneca, *Letters from a Stoic*, trans. Richard Mott Gummere (Enhanced Media, 2017), 25.

control; but as worry grows up, it lives and takes up residence in the mind. Over time, it slowly but surely begins building a house, one brick at a time. It might not come out and say, "Look at me! I'm the sum of all your worry, and I'm living here!" But over time, it builds.

It takes that one conversation, one critique, one circumstance that is out of your control, and it slowly adds it to the structure. A bit of anxiety here, a dash of fear there, and before we know it, worry is taking up a lot of real estate in our minds.

WHERE DID THAT THOUGHT COME FROM?

Worry thrives in our heads because it feasts on the future and things that have not yet come to pass. I'd guess that if you took ten minutes and wrote down everything you can think of that is currently worrying you, most of your list would be things that haven't happened yet. In fact, if you went back and wrote down things that worried you last week, or last month, or even within the last year, I'd guess that most of what would populate your list hasn't actually happened.

Why is that? It's because worry works best when it can convince you to spend your time fighting imaginary battles, therefore paralyzing you to the real work at hand. That's why you must do the work of taking back your mind.

If our goal is to be transformed and to fully take up our identity as a new creation, a loved son or a loved daughter of the King of the universe, we'll need to start by renewing our minds (Romans 12:2). We do that by following Paul's mandate in 2 Corinthians 10:5: to "take captive every thought."

As we take our thoughts captive, we slowly begin deconstructing the house that worry built. We begin taking away the stones and supports that anchor worry to our minds as we submit our fears and surrender our desire for control to Christ.

But if we're going to place a dagger through the heart of worry, it's not enough to tear down the strongholds worry has built in our minds. We need to remove and replace those thoughts with something else. That's where Philippians 4 comes in.

Paul told the Philippians that to not be anxious about anything, they needed a new story. A new narrative. New thoughts. They needed the *what ifs* to be transformed into *even ifs*.

They needed to replace the nightmares with things that were noble. They needed to replace the risks with things that were right. They needed to replace the panic with things that were pure.

That's the secret. It's the final step in driving the dagger into the heart of worry and walking away free, victorious, and unburdened by the weight of worry.

So how do you do that practically? You become very good at asking yourself this question: "Where did that thought come from?"

Say that out loud right now. Say it again. My prayer is that this simple question will become a consistent spark that empowers you to reject the narrative of worry and to reclaim the narrative of your Savior.

When you ask yourself the question, *Where did that thought come from?* you'll get an answer from one of two places: either from God, or from somewhere else. But how do you know what comes from God?

Paul told us in Philippians 4:8 that the things from God are true, noble, right, pure, lovely, admirable, excellent, and praiseworthy. You see where I'm going with this? If that isn't enough to identify the thought, look at the fruit of the Spirit from Galatians 5:22–23. Does the thought line up with that which is loving, joyous, peaceful, or patient?

If the answer is yes, keep that thought. If the answer is no, it doesn't line up, then you know it's time for a replacement.

This might sound like a lot of work. And you know what? It is. But remember, it's not ours to carry alone. Because of God's perfect love for us, He has given us a helper, His Spirit. Through the power of the Holy Spirit, we become competent (2 Corinthians 3:4–5) to carry out all the good works that God has created for us to walk in (Ephesians 2:10).

In the Old Testament, God gave His people the Mosaic law, and He commanded them to obey every statute and decree. He did this for two reasons: first, to show how holy and perfect He was. And second, to show how impossible it was for us to reach that standard of perfection.

In effect, God laid on the Israelites an impossibly heavy burden and said, "See, you can't carry this on your own.

You need a Savior." That's why God sent His own Son in the likeness of sinful man—to be a sin offering (Romans 8:3).

In doing so, God fulfilled the righteous requirement of the law in us, who no longer are bound to live according to the flesh and the anxieties that so commonly drag us down. We no longer live as slaves to those fears. No longer are we destined to spiral into a tunnel of control only to come out the other side with a mile-long list of worries.

Instead, God gave us a Spirit of adoption—His Spirit (Romans 8:15). Which is why Jesus can tell us: "Come to me, all you who are weary and burdened, and I will give you rest. Take my yoke upon you and learn from me, for I am gentle and humble in heart, and you will find rest for your souls. For my yoke is easy and my burden is light" (Matthew 11:28–30).

You won't drive the dagger of God's perfect love through the heart of worry unless you realize that through Christ, you have the power to do all things. Through Christ, you are a resurrected, new creation, no longer under the power of this world and its ways. You are free and perfectly loved, and as such, you can take back your mind, eliminating worry and accepting the easy and light yoke of your good and gracious Savior.

PRAYER

Father, please equip me with conviction and empower me by Your Spirit to dismantle the house of worry in my mind. I want to begin replacing each brick of anxiety with what is holy and pure. I desire to honor You with every thought, so I ask for Your strength to continue this pursuit. Put Your favor on the work of my hands and my mind and let flourish those thoughts that bring me life and bring You glory.

DISCUSSION AND REFLECTION QUESTIONS

1. Take a few minutes to write down any thoughts that are worrying you right now. Below each thought, write out a truth about God you can use to refute and replace that thought of worry.

_____

_____

_____

_____

_____

2. What inputs are constantly pushing thoughts of worry into your heart? Are there any streams you need to cut off if you are going to get serious about tearing down the house that worry built?

_____

_____

_____

_____

_____

3. Read Philippians 4:8. Pick one of the words Paul encouraged you to think about and write out a list of thoughts that relate to that word.

_____

_____

_____

_____

_____

4. What does it mean that you are a "new creation" in
   Christ (2 Corinthians 5:17)? What in your life has
   been made new?

_____

_____

_____

_____

_____

SEVEN

WHO NEEDS TO BE AWAKE ALL NIGHT?

Worry, in full force, can affect every area of our lives—our relationships, our work, our families, our motivations. It can even affect our sleep.

You may know this scene well: Suddenly, in the middle of the night, you are jarred awake. Something within startled you, and now you are fully conscious, your mind spinning with a situation that's been causing you a great deal of worry and consternation. You tried to sleep, but your mind couldn't downshift into rest mode. Now your heart and mind are racing. You glance over at the clock on the nightstand or reach for your smartphone. It's 2:27 A.M. Again! The pill you took to try to lull your body to sleep didn't stop the freight train of worry roaring down the tracks of your mind.

If this sounds familiar, you know what happens next. Nothing. If you're lucky, you'll be back to sleep in an hour or so. Or the tossing and turning could last until morning. And what will you have accomplished by overthinking and rehearsing and strategizing through the night? Not much.

When your alarm sounds, you'll pretty much be in the same situation you were in when you went to sleep the night before. Except now you're a little more tired and thinking a little less clearly.

A night of sound sleep may seem like a small thing, but it's a good picture for us as we head toward the finish line of winning the war on worry. When you think about a life characterized by peace, your mind likely jumps to someone who is restful. And few things are more restful than a good night of uninterrupted sleep.

God knows this, and that's why His Word says in Psalm

23:2, "He makes me lie down in green pastures." He provides rest for the weary. Psalm 4:8 says, "In peace I will lie down and sleep, for you alone, Lord, make me dwell in safety." One of the great rewards of winning the war on worry is that you no longer have to be subject to sleepless nights. That's not God's way. He Himself is up throughout the night so you don't have to be, and He's keeping you safe and at peace.

FIX YOUR GAZE HEAVENWARD

Our God is a God of peace, and He leads us toward rest if we will let Him. So how do we trade in fitful nights for faith-filled rest? First, we fix our gaze on our heavenly Father. The psalmist said it this way: "I have set the Lord continually before me; because He is at my right hand, I will not be shaken. Therefore my heart is glad and my glory rejoices; My flesh also will dwell securely" (Psalm 16:8–9 NASB 1995).

The writer of this psalm is David, the one who penned Psalm 23 and talked of having no fear in the middle of death valley. David knew all kinds of trouble, despair, and hardship. He knew what it was like to fail and to flee, to fight mighty armies and to be betrayed by those closest to him.

David knew that the starting point for a more peaceful night was keeping his gaze "always" on the Lord (Psalm 16:8, NIV). Some translations of this verse use the word *continually*. "I have set the LORD continually before me" (NASB 1995). In other words, this isn't something I do once in a while. It's the constant activity of recentering my thoughts and shifting my focus to get God in view. And when I do, three things happen.

First, my heart is glad. I have a shift in my emotions. Fear is replaced by a sense of confidence rooted in the reality that the Almighty is with me.

Second, I rejoice. Worship displaces worry as praise fills my mouth.

Third, my body rests securely. I lie down in the bed of steadfast hope, and I rest believing God is in control.

Right about now you may be thinking, *That sounds so idealistic . . . and unrealistic!* Maybe you've even tried to quote a favorite Scripture verse or say a prayer during the middle of the night, but to no avail.

Please don't throw in the towel just yet. God is fighting for you, and He will help you win whatever battle of worry you are facing.

So what's the key? The most important step in finding rest is focusing on the God you are continually setting before you. The Almighty One, the Maker of heaven and earth. Make every effort to make sure He is always at the forefront of your thoughts. We're not just talking about generic "God." You need to be more specific than that. Remember these key attributes of God when you focus on Him.

GOD IS AWAKE, ALERT, AND ABLE

We've already talked about the fact that He is a God of love, and that He is in love with you. And we've focused on the fact that He is good at being in control. But what else does He want you to notice? That He is awake, alert, and able!

WINNING THE WAR ON WORRY

The God who is ever before you is always awake. He's never been tired or weary. The Almighty has never once closed His eyes in sleep. "He who watches over you will not slumber; indeed, he who watches over Israel will neither slumber nor sleep" (Psalm 121:3–4).

Not only is God awake, but He is also alert. It's possible to be fully awake yet not be paying attention. God is both awake and zeroed in on your every need. In fact, He knows what you need long before you do. David prayed in Psalm 139:4, "Before a word is on my tongue you, LORD, know it completely." That means before I have a need that causes me to voice a prayer, God already knows about it. He sees the whole path ahead of me before I even take the next step.

This is why we celebrate the next facet of His character: He is able. What good would it do if God were awake and alert if He weren't able to do something about the things we are worrying about? Not only is God able, but He is also working on your behalf—whether you see it or not.

It's important to clarify that the fact that God is awake, alert, and able might not automatically mean that your circumstance pivots to your desired outcome. Yet focusing on these truths will help your peace of mind. Knowing God is going to be up all night will allow you to close your eyes and drift off to sleep. You will be able to release what you cannot control and wake up believing God has accomplished His purposes while you were asleep.

As you lie down at night, I encourage you to say to God:

Thank You that You will be awake all night. Thank You that You are watching over all that concerns me. I believe You are able to do exactly what You want to do. I need rest, so I will trust in You.

To take this approach is to be rooted in the realization that God is in control—awake, alert, and able 24/7.

To truly believe this is to say with the psalmist, "Unless the LORD builds the house, the builders labor in vain. Unless the LORD watches over the city, the guards stand watch in vain. In vain you rise early and stay up late, toiling for food to eat—for he grants sleep to those he loves" (Psalm 127:1–2). As we close, I want to leave you with one last weapon in the war on worry: a grateful heart.

THE POWER OF A GRATEFUL HEART

It's a scientific fact that gratitude positively affects mental health and reduces the anxiety that leads to worry. A recent publication found that "when we express gratitude and receive the same, our brain releases dopamine and serotonin, the two crucial neurotransmitters responsible for our emotions, and they make us feel 'good'. They enhance our mood immediately, making us feel happy from the inside."

This suggests that "by consciously practicing gratitude every day, we can help these neural pathways to strengthen themselves and ultimately create a permanent grateful and positive nature within ourselves."[1]

Thus, as Cicero believed, "gratitude is not only the greatest of virtues, but the parent of all the others."[2]

But the transformational power of a grateful heart is also a spiritual reality underscored throughout Scripture.

---

1. Madhuleena Roy Chowdhury, "The Neuroscience of Gratitude and How It Affects Anxiety and Grief," PositivePsychology.com, February 5, 2022, https://positivepsychology.com/neuroscience-of-gratitude.
2. M. Tullius Cicero, *For Plancius,* ed. C.D. Yongue, 33.80, http://www.perseus.tufts.edu/hopper/text?doc=Perseus%3Atext%3A1999.02.0020%3Atext%3DPlanc.%3Achapter%3D33.

When we revisit Philippians 4:6–7, we find gratitude at the core of the fight on worry: "Do not be anxious about anything, but in every situation, by prayer and petition, with thanksgiving, present your requests to God. And the peace of God, which transcends all understanding, will guard your hearts and your minds in Christ Jesus."

Did you notice it? *With thanksgiving.* We would all assume that prayer and petition are essential in the battle for peace of mind. Yet also in the mix is a grateful heart. The word *thanksgiving* in this verse means to be thankful for the grace of God.[3]

Worry causes us to have spiritual amnesia, making us forget that God is the One who has brought us through every trial and difficulty. Gratitude reminds us of His faithfulness, and His faithfulness boosts our confidence no matter the situation.

During one of the darkest periods in my life, when worry had compounded into a paralyzing season of depression, I dreaded the nightly 2:00 A.M. wake-up call from within the

---

3. "2170. Eucharistos," Strong's Greek: 2170. εὐχάριστος (Eucharistos)—thankful, accessed May 23, 2022, https://biblehub.com/greek/2170.htm.

recesses of an unsettled mind. I'd wake up feeling like a mountain had collapsed on my chest, suffocating life and hope. Months into the struggle, during a desperate night, I recalled a verse in Job that says God "gives songs in the night" (35:10).

That night I asked God to birth a spontaneous worship song in my heart, and He did. Though my heart was feeble and my soul was shredded, I sang in my mind: *Be still (my soul), there is a Healer. His love is deeper than the sea. His mercy is unending. His arms a refuge for the weak.*

I wasn't instantly healed overnight, but I was armed with a song of praise the next night when the temptation to lie awake in worry arrived.

Over time, that simple confession of confidence in God (along with a doctor's help and the encouragement of my community) pierced the darkness and led me back into the light.

Gratefulness is a torpedo that sinks worry. Gratitude opens the doorway for praise, and praise dispels fear. Worry and worship cannot be in our mouths at the same time. One always displaces the other.

As you place the Almighty consistently before you, thank Him. Do this daily. In fact, when you start your day, think of two or three things you are grateful for and praise Him. Over time, you'll notice a shift in your mindset and a change of heart. You'll notice your thankfulness leading to praise and your praise changing the landscape of your life.

PRAYER

Father, I just want to say thank You. Thank You for saving me. Thank You for seeing me when I was far off. Thank You for the power of Your cross to overcome every bit of darkness and despair. Thank You for being able when I am not, for being awake and alert and mindful of me. You are infinite and intimate, and I bow in adoration of You.

DISCUSSION AND REFLECTION QUESTIONS

1. What are you grateful for? Take some time to list out every single thing that comes to mind.

_____

_____

_____

_____

_____

2. Rest is a reaction to something that makes us feel safe. How do the power and authority of God help lead you to rest well?

_____

_____

_____

_____

_____

3. We counter spiritual amnesia by recalling what God has done for us in the past. What has He done for you that you can stand firm upon?

_____

_____

_____

_____

_____

4. What is the current soundtrack of your mind? Are you listening to songs of worship or songs of worry? What do they sound like?

_____

_____

_____

_____

_____

CONCLUSION

KEPT IN PERFECT PEACE

We've reached the end of our exploration of what it looks like to win the war on worry. With the ground we've covered in the previous chapters, I believe you have all you need to begin cultivating a peaceful heart and a confident mind.

As in most wars, things may not change dramatically for you overnight. Throughout history, major conflicts have traditionally been characterized by a series of battles or skirmishes that take place over an extended period of time, all of which culminate in what we know as war.

The same is true for you. You now have the proper tools to step into the fight and to stand your ground. There will be days when you'll get it right. When you'll trust in your identity as a loved son or daughter of God and when you practice gratitude—taking captive the lies of worry and replacing those thoughts with ones that are pure and lovely. And there will be days you'll feel like you're outnumbered or like you've made no progress in your mission.

Given the length of this fight and the likelihood of the highs and lows, I want to encourage you to focus both on the micro *and* the macro picture. Here's what I mean.

When you focus on the micro, you contextualize your battle to *today*. Right now. This moment, this minute, maybe even this hour. We know from James 4 that we aren't guaranteed tomorrow, and we've talked in earlier chapters about how future fixation is one of the weapons that worry wields. So let's make this practical. Focus on the micro picture. How can you win the next fight in front of you?

When you focus on the micro picture, you don't have time to look back and get bogged down by your previous fights. You don't have time to rest on your laurels or languish in your defeats. You only have eyes for this moment. *How can I take captive* this *thought? How can I replace* this *worry?* Don't look ahead. Don't look side to side. Look up. Fix your eyes on Jesus. Win this fight. Take this step. Claim this ground. Focus on the small picture.

Remember, though, the goal is to focus on *both* the micro and the macro picture. Here's the macro picture.

The war is already over. Jesus has already conquered sin, death, hell, and the grave. Remember how we outlined the operating system of the world? It begins with fear, but the macro picture is that Jesus has already defeated fear once and for all. It might still prowl around and act like a big, tough lion, but it's hollow. Its fangs aren't lethal and its sting is gone.

We've spent a lot of time digging into Romans 8, but turn once more with me to verse 15, which says, "The Spirit you received does not make you slaves, so that you live in fear again; rather, the Spirit you received brought about your adoption to sonship. And by him we cry, '*Abba*, Father.'"

For those who have put their faith in Jesus, we no longer need to fall back into fear. We are no longer bound by the ways of this world or the workings of the Enemy. We are freed. And more than that, we're placed into a new family—one where we can, with intimacy, call upon our Father and He will answer. The macro picture is that we are a part of a winning story. No matter what today holds, we can stand assured that on that final day, we will win the war on worry once and for all.

The macro picture of assurance fuels our micro picture of launching our assault on worry. The truth that the war is over should spur us to fight with all we have today, because freedom, hope, joy, peace, and refuge are not only available, but they are also our inheritance.

A STEP TOWARD FREEDOM

I'm praying that for many of you, a step toward freedom was taken over the last chapters. For some of you, a particular thought pattern was rewritten or a certain circumstance was recast in a new light. And for all of us, I'm praying that we realize that worry no longer gets the final word in the story God is writing for us.

We started this journey by comparing worry to the

barnacles that so often cling to the bottom of a ship. We looked at how when worry plagues our thoughts, it can feel like the extra weight that drags down a boat and slows down its speed. But throughout these last seven chapters, we've looked at specific, practical ways to strip worry of its power and to fix our eyes on the One who can actually keep us in perfect peace.

I know for me, this message has really changed the way I live and the way I go about my days. God has been working on my heart to win the war against worry for years now, and it's still a battle. But I'm confident that as I've seen Him move in my life, He is able and willing to move in yours as well.

Jesus has given you all you need for life and godliness (2 Peter 1:3). He has already won the war on worry, defeating death, hell, and the grave once and for all. As you go from here and venture into your day-to-day, keep these things in mind:

Worry is a lie from the Enemy. We can't necessarily stop him from talking, but we can choose who we listen to: the Enemy or our heavenly Father.

Worry will try to get you to focus on what you can control—to take matters into your own hands. Stand firm on the truth that Jesus both wants to and is able to carry what's worrying you.

Just because you aren't meant to be in control doesn't mean you shouldn't ever plan or be concerned. We should be wise stewards of what God has given us to hold, knowing that we win when we surrender His things back to Him.

Fear can lead to our desire to control, which fuels worry. But God's perfect love drives out fear. When we embrace His love, we move toward surrender and a life characterized by trust.

Ultimately, if we want to counter worry, we need to fix our eyes on Jesus. Start small, fight distractions, and begin by replacing anxious thoughts with thoughts that line up with the character and nature of God.

As we finish, remember that the peace of God—the one that Paul said surpasses all understanding—will guard your heart *and* your mind (Philippians 4:7). God is able to keep you from stumbling and to present you to Himself blameless and pure (Ephesians 5:27). You are a loved son or a loved daughter of the King of the universe. He is for you. He is with you. And in Him, you can win your war on worry and cultivate a peaceful heart and a confident mind.

ABOUT THE AUTHOR

Louie is the national-bestselling author of over a dozen books, including his newest releases, *Don't Give the Enemy a Seat at Your Table* and *At the Table with Jesus*, as well as *Goliath Must Fall, Indescribable: 100 Devotions About God and Science, The Comeback, The Air I Breathe, I Am Not but I Know I Am*, and others. As a communicator, Louie is widely known for messages such as "Indescribable" and "How Great Is Our God."